Music Is in the Air

Written by Ann Morris

Photographs by Ken Heyman

SCHOLASTIC INC.

New York   Toronto   London   Auckland   Sydney

Copyright © 1994 by Scholastic Inc.
All rights reserved. Published by Scholastic Inc.
Printed in the U.S.A.
ISBN 0-590-27540-2
ISBN 0-590-29346-X (meets NASTA specifications)

15   14   13   12   11   08   01 00 99 98 97

Music is in the air,

at home,

on the street,

in school,

at a concert,

on a boat,

in a marching band,

in a box,

at the park,

on a merry-go-round,

in a parade,

at a street fair,

on the grass,

in our ears!